To my Mother

This book is dedicated to the memory of my dear friend John Webb. He was a great man, a guiding light, always there in a time of need, a man you could trust and one whose inspiration is still with me.

'I have lived with Shades'

Poems and Prose by Thomas Hardy

Photographs by Philip Galvan

Ridgeway Publishing
Dorset. England

Foreword Copyright © Dr. James Gibson 1998

Published by

      Ridgeway Publishing
      29 White Cliff Mill St.
      Blandford Forum
      Dorset DT11 7 BQ
      England

All Photographs © Philip Galvan 1998

Printed in Great Britain by

      Epic Printing Services
      Epic House, Alington Avenue
      Dorchester, Dorset, DT1 1EX

ISBN 0-9533664-0-5

A donation from the sale of this book will be made to the "Friends of St. Juliot Church" in aid of their Roof Appeal

CONTENTS

CONTENTS

ACKNOWLEDGEMENTS

I am most grateful to the National Trust (Wessex Area); and to Mr & Mrs Andrew Leah and Mr & Mrs Terry Linee at Hardy's Cottage for their help and co-operation.

Hardy enthusiasts will know of the kindness and limitless enthusiasm of James and Helen Gibson, thank you to both of them for their generous time and constant encouragement.

I am gratefully indebted to John Truswell, Alan & Elke Burden and family, and good friend Caroline Harper for their generous financial support.

For their co-operation with regard to copyright I am most grateful to Macmillan Publishing.

The members of the Thomas Hardy Society have shown me fun and friendship and the value of the interaction of ideas and opinion. Their enthusiasm has inspired so many people throughout the world.

With regard to the preparation of text and computer expertise many thanks to Alan Brinded, and to the capable and friendly staff at Epic Print. Thanks also to Esther Ward at Paul Williams Photography, and to David Conway, for their professionalism in producing the final prints for the exhibition and book.

In March of 1998 I had the pleasure of visiting St. Juliot in Cornwall to capture those first emotions that Hardy must have felt in 1870 as he approached the Rectory for the first time. It was here that I was afforded the generous hospitality of Wing-Commander Gordon Bax and his delightful family.

For access to their beautiful properties I would like to thank Mr & Mrs Giles Sturdy at Trigon and Mr & Mrs Prideaux-Brune of Plumber Manor for their helpful co-operation.

The many photographers who visit Duckspool, like myself, owe a great deal to Peter and Sue Goldfield, whose inspiration and enthusiasm is infectious. Long may their Courses run and their food be "tasty" and "plentiful".

This book would not have been possible without the endless reading, typing, lengthy walks and boundless enthusiasm of Heather Shean, who has been a great right hand woman.

My sincere thanks to my friends and colleagues who, although not named individually, have contributed enormously to this book by their constant support and good humour.

Finally I must thank my good friend and confidante, Fiona, whose support for this venture has never wavered, even though many of the trips have been at the crack of dawn!

BLANDFORD FORUM,
DORSET.

JULY 1998.

FOREWORD

It has been well said that 'The creative photographer sets free the <u>human contents</u> of objects, and imparts humanity to the inhuman world around him.' This is certainly true of the photographs contained in this book. The art of Philip Galvan has much in common with the art of Thomas Hardy. Both try to create a lasting beauty out of the transient, to impress us with the continuity of past and present, and to impart humanity and some kind of meaning to the world they see around them.

'Seeing' is important to both of them. Part of Hardy's genius is found in his ability to describe his 'partly real, partly dream-country' in such a way that he gives his readers both a sense of timelessness and universality and what Desmond Hawkins calls 'a vividly detailed particularity of time and place.' Philip's photographs often aim at, and achieve, the same quality.

I have been immensely impressed by the manner in which the photographs reveal the photographer's sensitive understanding of Hardy, the novelist and poet. The photographs in this book are the kind of photographs Hardy himself might have taken if he had been born a century later. As so often in our cultural history, one art has produced a work of distinction in another.

It is appropriate that this book is published in the year 1998, the centenary of the first publication of 'Wessex Poems'. It offers a contribution and a celebration of the greatness and lasting qualities of Hardy's verse in visual interpretations.

James Gibson.

Cerne Abbas, June 1998.

INTRODUCTION

One of the many and most agreeable advantages of living in Dorset for over twenty years is the pleasure of being surrounded by Hardy's beloved Wessex.

Thomas Hardy's written word ignites the emotions of the common man and there is no doubting his sheer genius. It was Leslie Stephen who said *"He touched our hearts by showing his own"*.

Hardy takes you by the hand and gently leads you through the lilting rhythms and interlocking rhymes of everyday experiences.

It is a privilege to celebrate the Centenary of the publication of 'Wessex Poems' in 1898, the first of his eight books of verse. Five hundred copies were printed and following mixed reviews it was not reprinted until 1903. I have included a few of these poems which are considered to be amongst his greatest.

The selected poems reflect Hardy's early days at the cottage in Higher Bockhampton, the stimulating Egdon Heath and all the emotions experienced as a young architect in Dorchester and London. His verse tells us of the first visit to Cornwall in 1870 where he met Emma Lavinia Gifford, who became his first wife, and from whence he returned to Dorset with 'Magic in my eyes'. From the rectory of St. Juliot's Church, Nr. Boscastle, Hardy reveals the romance of his early days with Emma, walks along the windswept shoreline from the harbour to Beeny Cliff and beyond, and summer picnics along the tree-lined valley of the babbling Valency River.

Journeying in verse Hardy travels through his two year idyll at Sturminster Newton, followed by the somewhat joyless years at Max Gate, his home in Dorchester. Overcome with remorse at the death of Emma in 1912, the wife he had once loved so much, Hardy writes some of the most beautiful love poetry in the English language.

The passages of prose taken from a small but selective number of his novels were chosen because of their powerful descriptive imagery bringing, as Florence his second wife said, 'The expression as near to the thought as language would allow'. Photography in the latter part of the 19th century was still in its infancy, but Hardy reveals his 'photographic eye' capturing the landscape and spirit of the countryside in the places he knew so well. No mystery or emotion eluded him, the sights, the sound, the everchanging seasons. Hardy noticed them all.

At times the shades of pessimism cast lengthy shadows, but Hardy's work is made up of all life's realities, sadness and joy, hope and despair, and even humour is lightly sprinkled throughout his work. Hardy's death on January 11th 1928 saw the passing of one of the world's greatest writers. His heart was buried in the grave of his first wife in Stinsford Churchyard, his ashes in Poet's Corner, Westminster Abbey.

It is intended that 'I have lived with Shades' will serve as a gentle introduction to the poetry and prose of Hardy which teachers of English may use to whet the appetite of their students.

I can only hope that I have gone a little way to capturing the poet's vision as he himself would have wanted, and that through this 'introduction' those readers who have not yet tasted the genius of Thomas Hardy will want to read more of the novels and poetry for themselves.

As Philip Larkin once said "One can read him for years and still be surprised"

Philip Galvan

"I Have Lived With Shades"

I have lived with Shades so long,
And talked to them so oft,
Since forth from cot and croft
I went mankind among,
    That sometimes they
    In their dim style
    Will pause awhile
    To hear my say;

And take me by the hand,
And lead me through their rooms
In the To-be, where Dooms
Half-wove and shapeless stand:
    And show from there
    The dwindled dust
    And rot and rust
    Of things that were.

"Now turn," they said to me
One day: "Look whence we came,
And signify his name
Who gazes thence at thee." –
    – "Nor name nor race
    Know I, or can,"
    I said, "Of man
    So commonplace."

"He moves me not at all;
I note no ray or jot
Or rareness in his lot,
Or star exceptional.
    Into the dim
    Dead throngs around
    He'll sink, nor sound
    Be left of him."

"Yet," said they, "his frail speech,
Hath accents pitched like thine –
Thy mould and his define
A likeness each to each –
    But go! Deep pain
    Alas, would be
    His name to thee,
    And told in vain!"

....*"he touched our hearts by showing his own"*....

Leslie Stephen 1879

It was a long low cottage with a hipped roof of thatch, having dormer windows breaking up into the eaves, a chimney standing in the middle of the ridge and another at each end. The window-shutters were not yet closed, and the fire and candle-light within radiated forth upon the thick bushes of box and laurestinus growing in clumps outside, and upon the bare boughs of several codlin-trees hanging about in various distorted shapes, the result of early training as espaliers combined with careless climbing into their boughs in later years. The walls of the dwelling were for the most part covered with creepers, though these were rather beaten back from the doorway – a feature which was worn and scratched by much passing in and out, giving it by day the appearance of an old keyhole.

Under the Greenwood Tree
Chap. II

It was a long low cottage with a hipped roof of thatch....

Neutral Tones

We stood by a pond that winter day,
And the sun was white, as though chidden of God,
And a few leaves lay on the starving sod;
     – They had fallen from an ash, and were gray.

Your eyes on me were as eyes that rove
Over tedious riddles of years ago;
And some words played between us to and fro
     On which lost the more by our love.

The smile on your mouth was the deadest thing
Alive enough to have strength to die;
And a grin of bitterness swept thereby
     Like an ominous bird a-wing .....

Since then, keen lessons that love deceives,
And wrings with wrong, have shaped to me
Your face, and the God-curst sun, and a tree,
     And a pond edged with grayish leaves.

And the sun was white, as though chidden of God....

"I Look Into My Glass"

I look into my glass,
And view my wasting skin,
And say, "Would God it came to pass
My heart had shrunk as thin!"

For then, I, undistrest
By hearts grown cold to me,
Could lonely wait my endless rest
With equanimity.

But Time, to make me grieve,
Part steals, lets part abide;
And shakes this fragile frame at eve
With throbbings of noontide.

The Impercipient

(At a Cathedral Service)

That with this bright believing band
    I have no claim to be,
That faiths by which my comrades stand
    Seem fantasies to me,
And mirage-mists their Shining Land,
    Is a strange destiny.

Why thus my soul should be consigned
    To infelicity,
Why always I must feel as blind
    To sights my brethren see,
Why joys they've found I cannot find,
    Abides a mystery.

Since heart of mine knows not that ease
    Which they know; since it be
That He who breathes All's-Well to these
    Breathes no All's-Well to me,
My lack might move their sympathies
    And Christian charity!

I am like a gazer who should mark
    An inland company
Standing upfingered, with, "Hark! hark!
    The glorious distant sea!"
And feel, "Alas, 'tis but yon dark
    And wind-swept pine to me!"

Yet I would bear my shortcomings
    With meet tranquillity,
But for the charge that blessed things
    I'd liefer not have be.
0, doth a bird deprived of wings
    Go earthbound wilfully!

. . . .

Enough. As yet disquiet clings
    About us. Rest shall we.

The Self-Unseeing

Here is the ancient floor,
Footworn and hollowed and thin,
Here was the former door
Where the dead feet walked in.

She sat here in her chair,
Smiling into the fire:
He who played stood there,
Bowing it higher and higher.

Childlike, I danced in a dream;
Blessings emblazoned that day;
Everything glowed with a gleam;
Yet we were looking away!

Here is the ancient floor,
Footworn and hollowed and thin....

Where we are huddled none can trace....

The Levelled Churchyard

"O Passenger, pray list and catch
    Our sighs and piteous groans,
Half stifled in this jumbled patch
Of wrenched memorial stones!

"We late-lamented, resting here,
    Are mixed to human jam,
And each to each exclaims in fear,
'I know not which I am!'

"The wicked people have annexed
    The verses on the good;
A roaring drunkard sports the text
    Teetotal Tommy should!

"Where we are huddled none can trace,
    And if our names remain,
They pave some path or porch or place
    Where we have never lain!

"Here's not a modest maiden elf
    But dreads the final Trumpet,
Lest half of her should rise herself,
    And half some sturdy strumpet!

"From restorations of Thy fane,
    From smoothings of Thy sward,
From zealous Churchmen's pick and plane,
    Deliver us O Lord! Amen!"

When I Set Out for Lyonnesse

When I set out for Lyonnesse,
    A hundred miles away,
    The rime was on the spray,
And starlight lit my lonesomeness
When I set out for Lyonnesse
    A hundred miles away.

What would bechance at Lyonnesse
    While I should sojourn there
    No prophet durst declare,
Nor did the wisest wizard guess
What would bechance at Lyonnesse
    While I should sojourn there.

When I came back from Lyonnesse
    With magic in my eyes,
    All marked with mute surmise
My radiance rare and fathomless,
When I came back from Lyonnesse
    With magic in my eyes!

With magic in my eyes!...

a little dell lay like a nest at their feet....

Another oasis was reached; a little dell lay like a nest at their feet, towards which the driver pulled the horse at a sharp angle, and descended a steep slope which dived under the trees like a rabbit's burrow. They sank lower and lower.

'Endelstow Vicarage is inside here,' continued the man with the reins. 'This part about here is West Endelstow; Lord Luxellian's is East Endelstow, and has a church to itself. Pa'son Swancourt is the pa'son of both, and bobs backward and forward. Ah, well! 'tis a funny world'.

A Pair of Blue Eyes
Chap. II

I Found Her Out There

I found her out there
On a slope few see,
That falls westwardly
To the salt-edged air,
Where the ocean breaks
On the purple strand,
And the hurricane shakes
The solid land.

I brought her here,
And have laid her to rest
In a noiseless nest
No sea beats near.
She will never be stirred
In her loamy cell
By the waves long heard
And loved so well.

So she does not sleep
By those haunted heights
The Atlantic smites
And the blind gales sweep,
Whence she often would gaze
At Dundagel's famed head,
While the dipping blaze
Dyed her face fire-red;

And would sigh at the tale
Of sunk Lyonnesse,
As a wind-tugged tress
Flapped her cheek like a flail;
Or listen at whiles
With a thought-bound brow
To the murmuring miles
She is far from now.

Yet her shade, maybe,
Will creep underground
Till it catch the sound
Of that western sea
As it swells and sobs
Where she once domiciled,
And joy in its throbs
With the heart of a child.

Where the ocean breaks on the purple strand....

A Dream or No

Why go to Saint-Juliot? What's Juliot to me?
    Some strange necromancy
    But charmed me to fancy
That much of my life claims the spot as its key.

Yes. I have had dreams of that place in the West,
    And a maiden abiding
    Thereat as in hiding;
Fair-eyed and white-shouldered, broad-browed and brown-tressed.

And of how, coastward bound on a night long ago,
    There lonely I found her,
    The sea-birds around her,
And other than nigh things uncaring to know.

So sweet her life there (in my thought has it seemed)
    That quickly she drew me
    To take her unto me,
And lodge her long years with me. Such have I dreamed.

But nought of that maid from Saint-Juliot I see;
    Can she ever have been here,
    And shed her life's sheen here,
The woman I thought a long housemate with me?

Does there even a place like Saint-Juliot exist?
    Or a Vallency Valley
    With stream and leafed alley,
Or Beeny, or Bos with its flounce flinging mist?

The lonely edifice was black and bare, cutting up into the sky from the very tip of the hill. It had a square mouldering tower, owning neither battlement nor pinnacle, and seemed a monolithic termination, of one substance with the ridge, rather than a structure raised thereon. Round the church ran a low wall; over-topping the wall in general level was the graveyard; not as a graveyard usually is, a fragment of landscape with its due variety of chiaro-oscuro, but a mere profile against the sky, serrated with the outlines of graves and a very few memorial stones. Not a tree could exist up there: nothing but the monotonous gray-green grass.

A Pair of Blue Eyes
Chap. IV.

Beeny Cliff

O the opal and the sapphire of that wandering western sea,
And the woman riding high above with bright hair flapping free -
The woman whom I loved so, and who loyally loved me.

The pale mews plained below us, and the waves seemed far away
In a nether sky, engrossed in saying their ceaseless babbling say,
As we laughed light-heartedly aloft on that clear-sunned March day.

A little cloud then cloaked us, and there flew an irised rain,
And the Atlantic dyed its levels with a dull misfeatured stain,
And then the sun burst out again, and purples prinked the main.

- Still in all its chasmal beauty bulks old Beeny to the sky,
And shall she and I not go there once again now March is nigh,
And the sweet things said in that March say anew there by and by?

What if still in chasmal beauty looms that wild weird western shore,
The woman now is - elsewhere - whom the ambling pony bore,
And nor knows nor cares for Beeny, and will laugh there nevermore.

on that clear-sunned March day....

Under the Waterfall

"Whenever I plunge my arm, like this,
In a basin of water, I never miss
The sweet sharp sense of a fugitive day
Fetched back from its thickening shroud of gray
    Hence the only prime
    And real love-rhyme
    That I know by heart,
    And that leaves no smart,
Is the purl of a little valley fall
About three spans wide and two spans tall
Over a table of solid rock,
And into a scoop of the self-same block;
The purl of a runlet that never ceases
In stir of kingdoms, in wars, in peaces;
With a hollow boiling voice it speaks
And has spoken since hills were turfless peaks."

"And why gives this the only prime
Idea to you of a real love-rhyme?
And why does plunging your arm in a bowl
Full of spring water, bring throbs to your soul?"

"Well, under the fall, in a crease of the stone,
Though where precisely none ever has known,
Jammed darkly, nothing to show how prized,
And by now with its smoothness opalized,
    Is a drinking-glass:
    For, down that pass
    My lover and I
    Walked under a sky

Of blue with a leaf-wove awning of green,
In the burn of August, to paint the scene,
And we placed our basket of fruit and wine
By the runlet's rim, where we sat to dine;
And when we had drunk from the glass together,
Arched by the oak-copse from the weather,
I held the vessel to rinse in the fall,
Where it slipped, and sank, and was past recall,
Though we stooped and plumbed the little abyss
With long bared arms. There the glass still is.
And, as said, if I thrust my arm below
Cold water in basin or bowl, a throe
From the past awakens a sense of that time,
And the glass we used, and the cascade's rhyme.
The basin seems the pool, and its edge
The hard smooth face of the brook-side ledge,
And the leafy pattern of china-ware
The hanging plants that were bathing there.

"By night, by day, when it shines or lours,
There lies intact that chalice of ours,
And its presence adds to the rhyme of love
Persistently sung by the fall above.
No lip has touched it since his and mine
In turns therefrom sipped lovers' wine."

The purl of a runlet that never ceases....

The soil upon these high downs was left so untended that they were unenclosed for miles, except by a casual bank or dry wall, and were rarely visited but for the purpose of collecting or counting the flock which found a scanty means of subsistence thereon.

A Pair of Blue Eyes
Chap. XXII

TO·THE·DEAR·MEMORY·OF
EMMA·LAVINIA·HARDY·BORN·GIFFORD
WIFE·OF·THOMAS·HARDY·AUTHOR·&·SISTER
IN·LAW·OF·THE·REV·C·HOLDER·FORMERLY
INCUMBENT·OF·THIS·PARISH·BEFORE·HER
MARRIAGE·SHE·LIVED·AT·THE·RECTORY
1868-1873·CONDUCTED·THE·CHURCH·MUSIC
&·LAID·THE·FIRST·STONE·OF·THE·REBUILT
AISLE·&·TOWER·SHE·DIED·AT·DORCHESTER
1912·&·IS·BURIED·AT·STINSFORD·DORSET·
ERECTED·BY·HER·HUSBAND·1913·

The Marble Tablet

There it stands, though alas, what a little of her
    Shows in its cold white look!
Not her glance, glide, or smile; not a tittle of her
    Voice like the purl of a brook;
    Not her thoughts, that you read like a book.

It may stand for her once in November
    When first she breathed, witless of all;
Or in heavy years she would remember
    When circumstance held her in thrall;
    Or at last, when she answered her call!

Nothing more. The still marble, date-graven,
    Gives all that it can, tersely lined;
That one has at length found the haven
    Which every one other will find;
    With silence on what shone behind.

'Welcome to one of your ancestral mansions!' said Clare....

They drove by the level road along the valley to a distance of a few miles, and, reaching Wellbridge, turned away from the village to the left, and over the great Elizabethan bridge which gives the place half its name. Immediately behind it stood the house wherein they had engaged lodgings, whose exterior features are so well known to all travellers through the Froom Valley; once portion of a fine manorial residence, and the property and seat of a d'Urberville, but since its partial demolition a farm-house.

'Welcome to one of your ancestral mansions!' said Clare as he handed her down. But he regretted the pleasantry; it was too near a satire.

Tess of the d'Urbervilles
Chap. XXXIV

Tess's Lament

I.   I would that folk forgot me quite,
        Forgot me quite!
     I would that I could shrink from sight,
        And no more see the sun.
     Would it were time to say farewell,
     To claim my nook, to need my knell,
     Time for all to stand and tell
        Of my day's work as done.

II. Ah! dairy where I lived so long,
        I lived so long;
     Where I would rise up staunch and strong,
        And lie down hopefully.
     'Twas there within the chimney-seat
     He watched me to the clock's slow beat -
     Loved me, and learnt to call me Sweet,
        And whispered words to me.

III. And now he's gone; and now he's gone; ...
        And now he's gone!
     The flowers we potted perhaps are thrown
        To rot upon the farm.
     And where we had our supper-fire
     May now grow nettle, dock, and briar,
     And all the place be mould and mire
        So cozy once and warm.

IV. And it was I who did it all,
        Who did it all;
     'Twas I who made the blow to fall
        On him who thought no guile.
     Well, it is finished - past, and he
     Has left me to my misery,
     And I must take my Cross on me
        For wronging him awhile.

V.   How gay we looked that day we wed,
        That day we wed!
     "May joy be with ye!" they all said
        A-standing by the durn.
     I wonder what they say o'us now,
     And if they know my lot; and how
     She feels who milks my favourite cow,
     And takes my place at churn!

VI. It wears me out to think of it,
        To think of it;
     I cannot bear my fate as writ,
        I'd have my life unbe;
     Would turn my memory to a blot,
     Make every relic of me rot,
     My doings be as they were not,
        And gone all trace of me!

And gone all trace of me!

The towers of the notable ruin to be visited rose out of the furthermost shoulder of the upland as she advanced, its site being the slope and crest of a smoothly nibbled mount at the toe of the ridge she had followed. When observing the previous uncertainty of the weather on this side Ethelberta had been led to doubt if the meeting would be held here today, and she was now strengthened in her opinion that it would not by the total absence of human figures amid the ruins, though the time of appointment was past.

Extract from The Hand of Ethelberta
Chap. XXXI

*The towers of the notable ruin....rose out of
the furthermost shoulder of the upland....*

When Oats Were Reaped

That day when oats were reaped, and wheat was ripe,
    and barley ripening,
The road-dust hot, the bleaching grasses dry,
    I walked along and said,
While looking just ahead to where some silent people lie:

"I wounded one who's there, and now know well
    I wounded her;
But, ah, she does not know that she wounded me!"
    And not an air stirred,
Nor a bill of any bird; and no response accorded she.

and barley ripening....

The outskirts of this level water-meadow were diversified by rounded and hollow pastures, where just now every flower that was not a buttercup was a daisy. The river slid noiselessly as a shade, the swilling reeds and sedge forming a flexible palisade upon its moist brink. To the north of the mead were trees, the leaves of which were new, soft and moist, not yet having stiffened and darkened under summer sun and drought - their colour being yellow beside a green - green beside a yellow. From the recesses of this knot of foliage the loud notes of three cuckoos were resounding through the still air.

Far from the Madding Crowd
Chap. XIX

The river slid noiselessly as a shade....

a momentary glance into the little garden
Fellow- Townsmen

beyond the expanse of dark green leaves, was a small door
Far from the Madding Crowd

Here, in the valley, the world seems to be constructed upon a smaller and more delicate scale; the fields are mere paddocks, so reduced that from this height their hedgerows appear a network of dark green threads overspreading the paler green of the grass. The atmosphere beneath is languorous, and is so tinged with azure that what artists call the middle distance partakes also of that hue, while the horizon beyond is of the deepest ultramarine. Arable lands are few and limited; with but slight exceptions the prospect is a broad rich mass of grass and trees, mantling minor hills and dales within the major. Such is the Vale of Blackmoor.

Tess of the d'Urbervilles
Chap. II

Here, in the valley, the world seems to be constructed upon a smaller and more delicate scale....Such is the Vale of Blackmoor....

Wessex Heights

There are some heights in Wessex, shaped as if by a kindly hand
For thinking, dreaming, dying on, and at crisis when I stand,
Say, on Ingpen Beacon eastward, or on Wylls-Neck westwardly,
I seem where I was before my birth, and after death may be.

In the lowlands I have no comrade, not even the lone man's friend -
Her who suffereth long and is kind; accepts what he is too weak to mend:
Down there they are dubious and askance; there nobody thinks as I,
But mind-chains do not clank where one's next neighbour is the sky.

In the towns I am tracked by phantoms having weird detective ways -
Shadows of beings who fellowed with myself of earlier days:
They hang about at places, and they say harsh heavy things -
Men with a wintry sneer, and women with tart disparagings.

Down there I seem to be false to myself, my simple self that was,
And is not now, and I see him watching, wondering what crass cause
Can have merged him into such a strange continuator as this,
Who yet has something in common with himself, my chrysalis.

I cannot go to the great grey Plain; there's a figure against the moon,
Nobody sees it but I, and it makes my breast beat out of tune;
I cannot go to the tall-spired town, being barred by the forms now passed
For everybody but me, in whose long vision they stand there fast.

There's a ghost at Yell'ham Bottom chiding loud at the fall of the night,
There's a ghost in Froom-side Vale, thin-lipped and vague, in a shroud of white,
There is one in the railway train whenever I do not want it near,
I see its profile against the pane, saying what I would not hear.

As for one rare fair woman, I am now but a thought of hers,
I enter her mind and another thought succeeds me that she prefers;
Yet my love for her in its fulness she herself even did not know;
Well, time cures hearts of tenderness, and now I can let her go.

So I am found on Ingpen Beacon, or on Wylls-Neck to the west,
Or else on homely Bulbarrow, or little Pilsdon Crest,
Where men have never cared to haunt, nor women have walked with me,
And ghosts then keep their distance; and I know some liberty.

On Sturminster Foot-Bridge

(Onomatopoeic)

Reticulations creep upon the slack stream's face
    When the wind skims irritably past,
The current clucks smartly into each hollow place
That years of flood have scrabbled in the pier's sodden base:
    The floating-lily leaves rot fast.

On a roof stand the swallows ranged in wistful waiting rows,
    Till they arrow off and drop like stones
Among the eyot-withies at whose foot the river flows:
And beneath the roof is she who in the dark world shows
    As a lattice-gleam when midnight moans.

The Musical Box

Lifelong to be
Seemed the fair colour of the time;
That there was standing shadowed near
A spirit who sang to the gentle chime
Of the self-struck notes, I did not hear,
    I did not see.

Thus did it sing
To the mindless lyre that played indoors
As she came to listen for me without:
"0 value what the nonce outpours -
This best of life - that shines about
    Your welcoming!"

I had slowed along
After the torried hours were done,
Though still the posts and walls and road
Flung back their sense of the hot-faced sun,
And had walked by Stourside Mill, where broad
    Stream-lilies throng.

And I descried
The dusky house that stood apart,
And her, white-muslined, waiting there
In the porch with high-expectant heart,
While still the thin mechanic air
    Went on inside.

At whiles would flit
Swart bats, whose wings, be-webbed and tanned,
Whirred like the wheels of ancient clocks:
She laughed a hailing as she scanned
Me in the gloom, the tuneful box
    Intoning it.

Lifelong to be
I thought it. That there watched hard by
A spirit who sang to the indoor tune,
"0 make the most of what is nigh!"
I did not hear in my dull soul-swoon -
    I did not see.

.... by Stourside Mill, where broad stream-lilies throng.

Overlooking the River Stour

The swallows flew in the curves of an eight
    Above the river-gleam
    In the wet June's last beam:
Like little crossbows animate
The swallows flew in the curves of an eight
Above the river-gleam.

Planing up shavings of crystal spray
    A moor-hen darted out
    From the bank thereabout,
And through the stream-shine ripped his way;
Planing up shavings of crystal spray
A moor-hen darted out.

Closed were the kingcups; and the mead
    Dripped in monotonous green,
    Though the day's morning sheen
Had shown it golden and honeybee'd;
Closed were the kingcups; and the mead
Dripped in monotonous green.

And never I turned my head, alack,
    While these things met my gaze
    Through the pane's drop-drenched glaze,
To see the more behind my back .....
0 never I turned, but let, alack,
These less things hold my gaze!

.... and the mead dripped in monotonous green.

The Darkling Thrush

I leant upon a coppice gate
    When Frost was spectre-gray,
And Winter's dregs made desolate
    The weakening eye of day.
The tangled bine-stems scored the sky
    Like strings of broken lyres,
And all mankind that haunted nigh
    Had sought their household fires.

The land's sharp features seemed to be
    The Century's corpse outleant,
His crypt the cloudy canopy,
    The wind his death-lament.
The ancient pulse of germ and birth
    Was shrunken hard and dry,
And every spirit upon earth
    Seemed fervourless as I.

At once a voice arose among
    The bleak twigs overhead
In a full-hearted evensong
    Of joy illimited;
An aged thrush, frail, gaunt, and small,
    In blast-beruffled plume,
Had chosen thus to fling his soul
    Upon the growing gloom.

So little cause for carolings
    Of such ecstatic sound
Was written on terrestrial things
    Afar or nigh around,
That I could think there trembled through
    His happy good-night air
Some blessed Hope, whereof he knew
    And I was unaware.

When Frost was spectre-gray....

On a thyme-scented, bird-hatching morning in May, between two and three years after the return from Trantridge - silent reconstructive years for Tess Durbeyfield - she left her home for the second time.

Tess of the d'Urbervilles
Chap. XVI

On a thyme-scented, bird-hatching morning in May....

Who else had hair bay-red as yours....

To Lizbie Browne

I.   Dear Lizbie Browne,
      Where are you now?
      In sun, in rain? -
      Or is your brow
      Past joy, past pain,
      Dear Lizbie Browne?

II.   Sweet Lizbie Browne,
      How you could smile,
      How you could sing! -
      How archly wile
      In glance-giving,
      Sweet Lizbie Browne!

III.   And, Lizbie Browne,
      Who else had hair
      Bay- red as yours,
      Or flesh so fair
      Bred out of doors,
      Sweet Lizbie Browne?

IV.   When, Lizbie Browne,
      You had just begun
      To be endeared
      By stealth to one,
      You disappeared
      My Lizbie Browne!

V.   Ay, Lizbie Browne,
      So swift your life,
      And mine so slow,
      You were a wife
      Ere I could show
      Love, Lizbie Browne.

VI.   Still, Lizbie Browne,
      You won, they said,
      The best of men
      When you were wed....
      Where went you then,
      0 Lizbie Browne?

VII.   Dear Lizbie Browne,
      I should have thought,
      "Girls ripen fast,"
      And coaxed and caught
      You ere you passed,
      Dear Lizbie Browne!

VIII.   But, Lizbie Browne,
      I let you slip;
      Shaped not a sign;
      Touched never your lip
      With lip of mine,
      Lost Lizbie Browne!

IX   So, Lizbie Browne,
      When on a day
      Men speak of me
      As not, you'll say,
      "And who was he?" -
      Yes, Lizbie Browne!

An August Midnight

A shaded lamp and a waving blind,
And the beat of a clock from a distant floor:
On this scene enter - winged, horned, and spined -
A longlegs, a moth, and a dumbledore;
While 'mid my page there idly stands
A sleepy fly, that rubs its hands ....

Thus meet we five, in this still place,
At this point of time, at this point in space.
- My guests besmear my new-penned line,
Or bang at the lamp and fall supine.
"God's humblest, they!" I muse. Yet why?
They know Earth-secrets that know not I.
Max Gate, 1899.

In the Mind's Eye

That was once her casement,
     And the taper nigh,
Shining from within there,
     Beckoned, "Here am I!"

Now, as then, I see her
     Moving at the pane;
Ah; 'tis but her phantom
     Borne within my brain! -

Foremost in my vision
     Everywhere goes she;
Change dissolves the landscapes,
     She abides with me.

Shape so sweet and shy, Dear,
     Who can say thee nay?
Never once do I, Dear,
     Wish thy ghost away.

The Garden Seat

Its former green is blue and thin,
And its once firm legs sink in and in;
Soon it will break down unaware,
Soon it will break down unaware.

At night when reddest flowers are black
Those who once sat thereon come back;
Quite a row of them sitting there,
Quite a row of them sitting there.

With them the seat does not break down,
Nor winter freeze them, nor floods drown,
For they are as light as upper air,
They are as light as upper air!

Dead "Wessex" the Dog to the Household

Do you think of me at all,
    Wistful ones?
Do you think of me at all
     As if nigh?
Do you think of me at all
At the creep of evenfall,
Or when the sky-birds call
     As they fly?

Do you look for me at times,
    Wistful ones?
Do you look for me at times
    Strained and still?
Do you look for me at times,
When the hour for walking chimes,
On that grassy path that climbs
     Up the hill?

You may hear a jump or trot,
    Wistful ones,
You may hear a jump or trot -
    Mine, as 'twere -
You may hear a jump or trot
On the stair or path or plot;
But I shall cause it not,
    Be not there.

Should you call as when I knew you,
    Wistful ones,
Should you call as when I knew you,
    Shared your home;
Should you call as when I knew you,
I shall not turn to view you,
I shall not listen to you,
    Shall not come.

The Ageing House

When the walls were red
That now are seen
To be overspread
With a mouldy green,
A fresh fair head
Would often lean,
From the sunny casement
And scan the scene,
While blithely spoke the wind to the little sycamore tree.

But storms have raged
Those walls about,
And the head has aged
That once looked out;
And zest is suaged
And trust grows doubt,
And slow effacement
Is rife throughout,
While fiercely girds the wind at the long-limbed sycamore tree!

When showers betumble the chestnut spikes....

Weathers

This is the weather the cuckoo likes,
    And so do I;
When showers betumble the chestnut spikes,
    And nestlings fly:
And the little brown nightingale bills his best,
And they sit outside at the "Travellers' Rest",
And maids come forth sprig-muslin drest,
And citizens dream of the south and west,
    And so do I.

This is the weather the shepherd shuns,
    And so do I;
When beeches drip in browns and duns,
    And thresh, and ply;
And hill-hid tides throb, throe on throe,
And meadow rivulets overflow,
And drops on gate-bars hang in a row,
And rooks in families homeward go,
    And so do I.

Here stretch the downs, high and breezy and green, absolutely unchanged since those eventful days. A plough has never disturbed the turf, and the sod that was uppermost then is uppermost now. Here stood the camp; here are distinct traces of the banks thrown up for the horses of the calvary, and spots where the midden-heaps lay are still to be observed. At night, when I walk across the lonely place, it is impossible to avoid hearing, amid the scourings of the wind over the grass-bents and thistles, the old trumpet and bugle calls, the rattle of the halters; to help seeing rows of spectral tents and the impedimenta of the soldiery.

The Melancholy Hussar
Chap. I

Here stretch the downs, high and breezy and green....

Great Things

Sweet cyder is a great thing,
A great thing to me.
Spinning down to Weymouth town
By Ridgway thirstily,
And maid and mistress summoning
Who tend the hostelry:
0 cyder is a great thing,
A great thing to me!

The dance it is a great thing,
A great thing to me,
With candles lit and partners fit
For night-long revelry;
And going home with day-dawning
Peeps pale upon the lea:
0 dancing is a great thing,
A great thing to me!

Love is, yea, a great thing,
A great thing to me,
When, having drawn across the lawn
In darkness silently,
A figure flits like one a-wing
Out from the nearest tree:
O love is, yes, a great thing,
A great thing to me!

Will these be always great things,
Great things to me? ....
Let it befall that One will call,
"Soul, I have need of thee:"
What then? Joy-jaunts, impassioned flings,
Love, and its ecstasy,
Will always have been great things,
Great things to me!

Military Preparations on an Extended Scale

The chief incident that concerned the household at the mill was that the miller, following the example of all his neighbours, had become a volunteer, and duly appeared twice a week in a red, long-tailed military coat, pipe-clayed breeches, black cloth gaiters, a heel-balled helmet-hat with a tuft of green wool, and epaulettes of the same colour and material...

......'Now, I hope you'll have a little patience,' said the sergeant, as he stood in the centre of the arc, 'and pay strict attention to the word of command, just exactly as I give it out to ye; and if I should go wrong, I shall be much obliged to any friend who'll put me right again, for I have only been in the army three weeks myself, and we are all liable to mistakes.'

'So we be, so we be,' said the line heartily.

' 'Tention, the whole, then. Poise fawlocks! Very well done!'

'Please, what must we do that haven't got no fire-locks!' said the lower end of the line in a helpless voice.

'Now, was ever such a question! Why, you must do nothing at all, but think *how* you'd poise 'em *if* you had 'em. You middle men, that are armed with hurdle-sticks and cabbage-stumps just to make-believe, must of course use 'em as if they were the real thing. Now then, cock fawlocks! Present! Fire! (Pretend to, I mean, and the same time throw yer imagination into the field o' battle.) Very good - very good indeed; except that some of you were a *little* too soon, and the rest a *little* too late.'

'Please, sergeant, can I fall out, as I am master-player in the choir, and my bass-viol strings won't stand at this time o' year, unless they be screwed up a little before the passon comes in?'

'How can you think of such trifles as church-going at such a time as this, when your own native country is on the point of invasion?' said the sergeant sternly. 'And, as you know, the drill ends three minutes afore church begins, and that's the law, and it wants a quarter of an hour yet. Now, at the word *Prime*, shake the powder (supposing you've got it) into the priming-pan, three last fingers behind the rammer; then shut your pans, drawing your right arm nimble-like towards your body. I ought to have told ye before this, that at *Hand your katridge,* seize it and bring it with a quick motion to your mouth, bite the top well off, and don't swaller so much of the powder as to make ye hawk and spet instead of attending to your drill. What's that man a-saying of in the rear rank?'

'Please, sir, 'tis Anthony Cripplestraw, wanting to know how he's to bite off his katridge, when he haven't a tooth left in's head?'

'Man! Why, what's your genius for war? Hold it up to your right-hand man's mouth, to be sure, and let him nip it off for ye. Well, what have you to say, Private Tremlett? Don't ye understand English?'

'Ask yer pardon, sergeant; but what must we infantry of the awkward squad do if Boney comes afore we get our firelocks?'

'Take a pike, like the rest of the incapables. You'll find a store of them ready in the corner of the church tower. Now then - Shoulder-r-r-r.'

The Trumpet-Major
Chap.XXIII

It was a bright silent evening at the beginning of September when Smith again set foot in the little town. He felt inclined to linger awhile upon the quay before ascending the hills, having formed a romantic intention to go home by way of her house, yet not wishing to wander in its neighbourhood till the evening shades should sufficiently screen him from observation.

And thus waiting for night's nearer approach, he watched the placid scene, over which the pale luminosity of the west cast a sorrowful monochrome, that became slowly embrowned by the dusk.

A Pair of Blue Eyes
Chap. XXV

It was a bright silent evening at the beginning of September....

It was about eleven o'clock on this day that Mrs. Yeobright started across the heath towards her son's house, to do her best in getting reconciled with him and Eustacia, in conformity with her words to the reddleman. She had hoped to be well advanced in her walk before the heat of the day was at its highest, but after setting out she found that this was not to be done. The sun had branded the whole heath with his mark, even the purple heath-flowers having put on a browness under the dry blazes of the few preceding days. Every valley was filled with air like that of a kiln, and the clean quartz sand of the winter water-courses, which formed summer paths, had undergone a species of incineration since the drought had set in.

The Return of the Native
The Closed Door - Chap. V

The sun had branded the whole heath with his mark....

The Walk

  You did not walk with me
  Of late to the hill-top tree
      By the gated ways,
      As in earlier days;
      You were weak and lame,
      So you never came,
And I went alone, and I did not mind,
Not thinking of you as left behind.

  I walked up there today
  Just in the former way;
      Surveyed around
      The familiar ground
      By myself again:
      What difference, then?
Only that underlying sense
Of the look of a room on returning thence.

You did not walk with me of late to the hill-top tree....

Beneath them a captive sheep lay panting....

Here the shearers knelt, the sun slanting in upon their bleached shirts, tanned arms, and the polished shears they flourished, causing these to bristle with a thousand rays strong enough to blind a weak-eyed man. Beneath them a captive sheep lay panting, quickening its pants as misgiving merged in terror, till it quivered like the hot landscape outside.

This picture of to-day in its frame of four hundred years ago did not produce that marked contrast between ancient and modern which is implied by the contrast of date. In comparison with cities, Weatherbury was immutable. The citizen's *Then* is the rustic's *Now*. In London, twenty or thirty years ago are old times; in Paris ten years, or five; in Weatherbury three or four score years were included in the mere present, and nothing less than a century set a mark on its face or tone. Five decades hardly modified the cut of a gaiter, the embroidery of a smock-frock, by the breadth of a hair. Ten generations failed to alter the turn of a single phrase. In these Wessex nooks the busy outsider's ancient times are only old; his old times are still new; his present is futurity.

Far from the Madding Crowd
Chap. XXII

Christmas had passed. Dreary winter with dark evenings had given place to more dreary winter with light evenings. Rapid thaws had ended in rain, rain in wind, wind in dust. Showery days had come - the season of pink dawns and white sunsets; and people hoped that the March weather was over.

The Trumpet-Major
Chap.XXIII

Rapid thaws had ended in rain ....

Of all spots on the bleached and desolate upland this was the most forlorn....

At length the road touched the spot called 'Cross-in-Hand.' Of all spots on the bleached and desolate upland this was the most forlorn. It was so far removed from the charm which is sought in landscape by artists and view-lovers as to reach a new kind of beauty, a negative beauty of tragic tone. The place took its name from a stone pillar which stood there, a strange rude monolith, from a stratum unknown in any local quarry, on which was roughly carved a human hand. Differing accounts were given of its history and purport. Some authorities stated that a devotional cross had once formed the complete erection thereon, of which the present relic was but the stump; others that the stone as it stood was entire, and that it had been fixed there to mark a boundary or place of meeting. Anyhow, whatever the origin of the relic, there was and is something sinister, or solemn, according to mood, in the scene amid which it stands; something tending to impress the most phlegmatic passer-by.

Tess of the d'Urbervilles
Chap. XLV

The oat-harvest began, and all the men were a-field under a monochromatic Lammas sky, amid the trembling air and short shadows of noon. Indoors nothing was to be heard save the droning of blue-bottle flies; out-of-doors the whetting of scythes and the hiss of tressy oat-ears rubbing together as their perpendicular stalks of amber-yellow fell heavily to each swath. Every drop of moisture not in the men's bottles and flagons in the form of cider was raining as perspiration from their foreheads and cheeks. Drought was everywhere else.

Far from the Madding Crowd
Chap. XXXIII

under a monochromatic Lammas sky....

I lie uncaring, slumbering peacefully....

"Regret Not Me"

Regret not me;
Beneath the sunny tree
I lie uncaring, slumbering peacefully.

Swift as the light
I flew my faery flight;
Ecstatically I moved, and feared no night.

I did not know .
That heydays fade and go,
But deemed that what was would be always so.

I skipped at morn
Between the yellowing corn,
Thinking it good and glorious to be born.

I ran at eves
Among the piled-up sheaves,
Dreaming, "I grieve not, therefore nothing grieves."

Now soon will come
The apple, pear, and plum,
And hinds will sing, and autumn insects hum.

Again you will fare
To cider-makings rare,
And junketings; but I shall not be there.

Yet gaily sing
Until the pewter ring
Those songs we sang when we went gipsying.

And lightly dance
Some triple-timed romance
In coupled figures, and forget mischance;

And mourn not me
Beneath the yellowing tree;
For I shall mind not, slumbering peacefully.

The trees stood in an attitude of intentness, as if they waited longingly for a wind to come and rock them. A startling quiet overhung all surrounding things so completely, that the crunching of the waggon-wheels was as a great noise, and small rustles, which had never obtained a hearing except by night, were distinctly individualized.

Far from the Madding Crowd
Chap. XLII

The trees stood in an attitude of intentness....

Afterwards

When the Present has latched its postern behind my tremulous stay,
    And the May month flaps its glad green leaves like wings,
Delicate-filmed as new-spun silk, will the neighbours say,
    "He was a man who used to notice such things"?

If it be in the dusk when, like an eyelid's soundless blink,
    The dewfall-hawk comes crossing the shades to alight
Upon the wind-warped upland thorn, a gazer may think,
    "To him this must have been a familiar sight."

If I pass during some noctural blackness, mothy and warm,
    When the hedgehog travels furtively over the lawn,
One may say, "He strove that such innocent creatures should come to no harm,
    But he could do little for them; and now he is gone. "

If, when hearing that I have been stilled at last, they stand at the door,
    Watching the full-starred heavens that winter sees,
Will this thought rise on those who will meet my face no more,
    "He was one who had an eye for such mysteries"?

And will any say when my bell of quittance is heard in the gloom,
    And a crossing breeze cuts a pause in its outrollings,
Till they rise again, as they were a new bell's boom,
    "He hears it not now, but used to notice such things"?

"He was one who had an eye for such mysteries....."

Thomas Hardy 1840 - 1928

Photographic Locations